THE FOUR NOBLE TRUTHS

THE FOUR NOBLE TRUTHS

by Venerable Gen Lobsang Gyatso
Director, Institute of Buddhist Dialectics

Translated by Venerable Sherab Gyatso

Snow Lion Publications
Ithaca, New York

Snow Lion Publications
P.O. Box 6483
Ithaca, New York 14851
USA

Printed in U.S.A.

ISBN 1-55939-027-1

Library of Congress Cataloging-in-Publication Data
Blo-bzań-rgya-mtsho, Phu-kha 'Dge-bśes
  The four noble truths / by Lobsang Gyatso : translated by Sherab
Gyatso.
    p.   cm.
  Includes bibliographical references and index.
  ISBN 1-55939-027-1
  1. Four Noble Truths.   I. Title.
BQ4230.B56   1994
294.3'422—dc20   94–2267
                                                              CIP

Contents

List of Figures

Acknowledgments

This material consists of the teachings given by Venerable Gen Lobsang Gyatso, Principal of the Institute of Buddhist Dialectics in Dharamsala, India in October, 1988. Venerable Sherab Gyatso served as translator for these teachings. He also prepared the Appendices and much of the Glossary. Venerable Kalsang Damdul, Secretary of the Institute, clarified many points and assisted in the editing. Their generosity and kindness made this effort possible.

The section of Chapter 4 dealing with the twelve links of dependent origination is based on teachings at Tushita Institute. These teachings were also given by Venerable Lobsang Gyatso and translated by Venerable Sherab Gyatso. However, the presentation here was condensed from a considerably longer transcript. Venerable Geshe Lobzang Tsetan assisted in clarifying the sequence of the twelve links. Venerable Graham Woodhouse reviewed the entire manuscript for proper terminology and made many valuable suggestions. William Magee reviewed the manuscript for accuracy and clarity and made many valuable suggestions. Venerable Tenzin Tsepak and Travis McCauley's efforts were invaluable in clarifying the section on emptiness. Jeff Cox and Sidney Piburn's interest made publication of this work possible. Susan Kyser's careful copy editing contributed greatly to the clarity and consistency of the manuscript. Much appreciation is also due to Rebecca Raupp of the Word Processing Center at Wayne State University for de-bugging an apparently hopeless disk and entering last-minute manuscript changes. Much gratitude is owed to all these people for their efforts in behalf of this endeavor.

Any errors or inadequacies in this presentation are based entirely on my own inadequacies in transcribing or condensing these teachings.

It is my sincere hope that these generous teachings will be beneficial to others.

Effie S. Hanchett
July 3, 1990

Venerable Lobsang Gyatso

Photo: Robert Geyer

1 Introduction

After his enlightenment Buddha Shakyamuni turned the First Wheel of Dharma, teaching the Four Noble Truths to the five disciples. The first two truths present the way in which sentient beings migrate into samsara (cycle of compulsive rebirth and suffering). The second two truths present the way in which they can release themselves from that cycle of suffering.

BACKGROUND

The discourse on the Four Noble Truths is regarded as both the essence and the outline of Buddhism. In dependence upon the first two truths, that is, the Truth of Suffering and the Truth of the Origin of Suffering, one can understand how sentient beings wander into samsara. In order to release oneself from suffering, one must realize the second two truths: the Truth of Cessation and the Truth of the Path.

The Four Noble Truths are called truths because they can be experienced and realized as taught by the Buddha. In fact, during Shakyamuni Buddha's time, many of his followers did reach arhatship and other realizations through practicing the Four Noble Truths. If one is able to practice, one can be sure to attain realizations.

13

By knowing the Four Noble Truths, one can attain clear realization of the ultimate reality of phenomena and thereby eliminate delusions. It can be said, therefore, that the Four Noble Truths accord with reality. For example, if you bought land, and tried to raise crops for the first time, if your experience in fertilizing, planting and harvesting fit with what you had been told, then you would know you had been told the truth. Similarly, if people outside Tibet were told of the political, cultural and religious oppression in Tibet, they might not believe what they were told unless they went to Tibet and saw the same things with their own eyes. If they did go, and what they saw was consistent with what they had been told, only then they would know they had been told the truth.

In the time of Shakyamuni Buddha, his followers had great experience of suffering and the causes of suffering. It did not take much to see that the first two Noble Truths were consistent with reality. In this era, people are less aware of suffering and its causes. Suffering is not seen as the effect of ignorance, attachment and delusion. Nor are these causes given much attention in thinking about suffering. Even if these causes are studied, they are not integrated with experience. Rather, they are considered from a purely academic point of view.

These Four Noble Truths are called noble truths because they are of Aryas or Superior Beings. This is because they are directly realized only by Aryas, that is, persons with superior attainments.

In summary, the Four Noble Truths were presented by Buddha Shakyamuni as the first teachings after his enlightenment. They are based on valid reasoning and supported by experience. Rather than becoming less confident with increased study, one becomes more confident in the importance and efficacy of these teachings.

THE FOUR NOBLE TRUTHS

Three issues must be addressed in presenting the Four Noble Truths. They are: (1) What are the Four Noble Truths? What content do they present? (2) How did the Buddha teach them? (3) Are these teachings of the Four Noble Truths actually consistent with reality or not?

These three questions will be dealt with together. That is, (1) the content, (2) the way in which it was presented, and (3) the fit of the content with reality will be discussed together for each of the Four Noble Truths.

Buddha first spoke of true suffering, stating "this is the Arya's Noble Truth of Suffering." The meaning of this is that all contaminated aggregates[1] and samsara are in the nature of suffering. This teaching is consistent with reality as seen by Aryas (Superior Beings) who are able to see the nature of suffering directly. They realize the suffering of others with direct perception.

Direct perception differs from inferential cognition in that inferential cognition requires a generic image (such as that provided by a map), whereas direct, valid perception does not.[2] Perceiving an object with inferential cognition is somewhat distant from the reality perceived, whereas direct valid perception places no intermediate image between the perceiver and the perceived. None of the vividness of perception is lost, as may occur with memory.

The First Noble Truth defines suffering. The Second Noble Truth states, "This is the truth of the cause of suffering." This means that negative karma and afflictive emotions are the sources of suffering. These two truths explain how sentient beings wander in samsara. The first two truths are interdependent in that the First Noble Truth defines suffering and describes the essence of sentient beings (contaminated aggregates) and their environment (samsara) as producing suffering. The Second Noble Truth specifies the source of suffering as karmic action and afflictive emotion. Among them ignorance is known as the root of all afflictive emotions and karmic action. The First Noble Truth is presented in Chapter 2. The Second Noble Truth is discussed in Chapter 3.

2 The First Noble Truth: The Truth of Suffering

The First Noble Truth addresses suffering. Suffering can be divided into two categories: (1) the suffering of sentient beings, and (2) the suffering of the environment. The suffering of the environment refers to the place in which suffering occurs. Both sentient beings and the environment have the nature of suffering.

THE ENVIRONMENT

There are six divisions of the environment in which sufferings occur. Buddhism explains existence as consisting of six realms. These realms are used as the basis for meditation on suffering. As a result of this meditation, one becomes disgusted by suffering and develops a strong determination to get out of cyclic existence (samsara). This determination is termed "a mind of definite emergence" (or a mind of renunciation). The six realms are named according to the kinds of beings that inhabit them: (1) gods, (2) demi-gods, (3) humans, (4) animals, (5) hungry spirits, and (6) hell beings.

Whether or not one accepts these six realms, without understanding them as set forth in Buddhism one cannot develop the mind that wishes to turn away from these sufferings. This mind of renunciation serves as the basis for liberation. It is said that as long as you are unable to understand how you are experiencing suffering in samsara yourself, you are not able to see how other sentient beings are chained in samsara. Therefore, you are not able to generate the compassion wishing other sentient beings to be freed from samsara.

SENTIENT BEINGS

Sentient beings are divided into two categories: (1) those with delusions and (2) those without delusions. Those sentient beings with delusions are included within true suffering: those sentient beings without delusions are not. In the same way, the environment in which we live, since it is the product of delusions, is also true suffering. However, Buddha's pure lands are not true suffering, for they are not the product of delusions but are merely the appearance of Buddha's wisdom.

The person living in the environment of suffering experiences suffering due to having various delusions. Persons and other sentient beings are said to be in the nature of suffering. They are both the experiencer and the experience of suffering. Suffering is not separate from them. They *are* true suffering.

TRUE SUFFERING

True suffering differs from suffering in that true suffering is in the *nature* of suffering. The aggregates of body and mind are in the nature of suffering. Both sentient beings and the environment have the nature of suffering, and are, therefore, called true suffering. They are not only the feeling of suffering.

True suffering is divided into three categories: (1) the suffering of suffering, (2) the suffering of change, and (3) pervasive suffering.

THE SUFFERING OF SUFFERING

The suffering of suffering is the obvious discomfort one undergoes in the experience of suffering.

THE SUFFERING OF CHANGE

Feelings of suffering change into those of happiness. Feelings of happiness change into suffering. Both arise in dependence upon internal and external causes which change. For example, we see food as pleasurable, but if we eat too much, then it causes suffering. When we are young, we see our bodies as a source of pleasure. As we become older, the same body becomes a source of suffering.

Just as a wave is always changing, so the nature of suffering is always to change. It may be experienced as pleasure or as suffering, but it arises from the same source. Pleasure arises from suffering. Seeing pleasure as happiness constitutes suffering.

When someone who is carrying a big load of rice on his back undergoes suffering while carrying it, and feels relief when it is set down, that is the suffering of change. The person still has to pick it up again and continue on. If someone is elected to high office, that person feels great happiness. However, concerns about the responsibilities, demands and conflicts of that office soon arise and act as the basis of suffering.

The whole process, the whole of existence, is seen as an ocean of suffering. Pain and pleasure are of the same nature. Although they look different at different times, they both arise from the same sea of delusion and karmic action. Pleasure or pain, one or the other, arises and then falls back into the ocean. Thus we can conclude that pleasure and pain within the ocean of samsara are basically suffering, and dissolve into suffering.

This becomes evident in the wide variety of sudden changes of experience depicted in films. Love and hatred, happiness and family strife, peace and war, follow each other in rapid succession. The continuous change, although exaggerated in films, is characteristic of life in general.

PERVASIVE SUFFERING

The third type of suffering is pervasive suffering. The Tibetan expression for pervasive suffering includes three words. The first word means to pervade. The second word means arising in dependence on the meeting of many causes and conditions. The final word means suffering. So, in essence, we should realize that the five aggregates of sentient beings arise from many causes and conditions. They are the medium of our present suffering and the causes for our future suffering. This form of suffering pervades all of existence.

THE FIVE AGGREGATES

All sentient beings, except those in the formless realms,[1] are made up of five aggregates. Those beings in the formless realms have only four aggregates. Those sentient beings made up of five aggregates are in the nature of suffering. There is nothing other than these five aggregates, and they are all in the nature of suffering.

The five aggregates are:

(1) *Form:* the physical body of sentient beings. It includes bone, flesh, blood and so forth.

(2) *Feeling:* that mental factor which feels and experiences either pleasure, pain or neutral feeling.

(3) *Discrimination:* a mental factor whose main function is to discriminate and comprehend the object without mistaking it with others.

(4) *Compositional factors:* those mental factors whose main function is to tie the object with the mind and to determine the object of use. Their function is to direct the mind toward an object of attention, to maintain or continue that attention and/or to change the focus of attention, and to continue or alter that focus.

(5) *Consciousness:* includes all the types of sense consciousness (eye, ear, nose, tongue, and body consciousness). Each of these sense consciousnesses is connected to its appropriate sense basis.

All ordinary beings are pervaded by having these five aggregates. (However, there are some beings in the highest realms who temporarily do not have feelings of suffering. Their experience is basically neutral.) There are also some occasions when ordinary beings do not have feelings of suffering. However, this is only temporary, and is changeable in that the lack of feelings of suffering does not last forever. Every being, however, is pervaded by the aggregates, and does have feeling in the sense of experience which is either pleasurable, unpleasurable or neutral. Pleasurable and unpleasurable experiences are based on delusion.

The five aggregates act as the basis for the sufferings sentient beings undergo. All of the different sufferings which they experience arise in dependence upon these aggregates through the power of delusions and karmic action. Birth in human form occurs due to delusions and the actions based on these delusions (see Chapter 3). This, in turn, acts as the basis for further sufferings. The whole being, body and mind, serves as the basis for those sufferings. All the feelings we experience are included within the aggregates.

A person's aggregates include all the different sufferings. All the sufferings are included within the aggregates, in the sense that the sufferings one experiences are not separate from the aggregates. They are not outside oneself. Someone who did not have contaminated aggregates would not experience suffering because s/he would be free from the bases of suffering. It is necessary to have contaminated aggregates in order to experience suffering.

By analogy, once a fish who has been free in the ocean is caught in a net, there is no way out. Until the fish is pulled out of the water, there is no way out of the net. Being caught in the net acts as the basis for its suffering. All of the fish's sufferings can be included within that. If the fish had never entered the net, it would not have to experience the sufferings. The same thing is true of beings in the six migrations or realms. Once we have adopted these contaminated aggregates, they act as the basis for the situation. Without having adopted the aggregates, there is no suffering.

THE FOUR TYPES OF SUFFERING

The four types of suffering—birth, sickness, aging and death—clearly illustrate how the aggregates act as the source of suffering.

BIRTH

Through the force of cooperation of delusion and karmic action, we have taken birth into samsara countless times and have experienced unimaginable suffering. Unless we cut the root of delusion and karma, we are sure again to take rebirth in samsara and go on experiencing suffering into the future.

Birth, propelled by delusions and karmic actions, is the door to all the other sufferings. Buddhists propound that there is future life, but there are many people who don't believe in future lives. If we examine these two views impartially, we find that there are more valid logical reasons for accepting the existence of future lives than for not doing so. The only reason given for not accepting the existence of future lives is that we have not seen them. We should prepare for future lives before it is too late, by putting effort into the elimination of delusion and negative karmic action.

SICKNESS

The body is a very fragile thing. It is continuously meeting with conditions which produce suffering. Even slight changes in temperature cause the body a great deal of harm, so we go to great lengths to try to protect our body. However, no one can avoid illness. It is impossible to spend one's entire life without ever getting ill. One is surrounded by the conditions which produce illness.

AGING

The nature of the aggregates is not only to be changing, but to be deteriorating. The body will eventually fall apart. So, in taking on a body, one has taken on the main cause for aging. As soon as one is born, one has a body which will age. We undergo a great deal of physical and mental suffering because of the process of aging.

DEATH

The experience of suffering which is associated with death is the result of having physical aggregates which the mind must be separated from at death. Because we have to part from the physical aggregates, both mental and physical suffering occur during the process of dying.

Here we are mainly concentrating on our body, although other aggregates are changing moment by moment. Aging here means getting closer to death. So the moment we take birth, we undergo the process of aging. But through meditation, we can overcome death.[2]

SUMMARY

In summary, there are two categories of true suffering: the environment and the beings themselves. It is only the sentient beings who actually experience suffering. However, because the relationship between the beings and the environment causes suffering, both the beings and the environment are said to have the nature of suffering. If we speak in terms of ultimate cause, both beings and environment arise from the karmic actions induced by ignorance.

3 The Second Noble Truth: The Origins of Suffering

The Second Noble Truth addresses the causes of the suffering which pervades sentient beings and their environment.

In Buddhism, there are said to be two causes of suffering: (1) karma (action) and (2) delusion. However, all of the karmic causes for suffering can be traced back to delusion. Karma and delusion are said to be the true origins of suffering. The term "true" has the same meaning as described in Chapter 1. That is, the way it is described is in accord with the real situation. The term "origins" (the source of every suffering) indicates that delusion and karmic actions are the root of every suffering.

The First Teaching (or First Turning of the Wheel of Dharma given by the Buddha) presented the fact of suffering. It leads to the questions "Why is there suffering?" and "Where do sufferings arise from?"

The Second Noble Truth is that of the true sources, the origins of suffering. Again, as described above, those beings who have traveled the path are able to directly realize, and therefore recognize, the teachings as true. Until one has had direct experience of them, one cannot say that they are true. However, the teachings are also true from the point of view of beings who have cognized them with inferential cognition.

As an analogy, if a clairvoyant told someone that they were going to contract a serious illness in three years, the person might believe that what they said was probably true, but some doubt would remain in their mind. If, after the three years had passed, the person actually contracted the illness, then the statement becomes true from that person's point of view. Similarly, the Four Noble Truths were first set forth by Buddha. His followers then practiced them, and when their practices were complete, they were able to say, "This is the truth."

THE ORIGINS OF SUFFERING

Karma and delusions are the source of suffering. Because the aggregates act as the basis for suffering in many ways, they are also said to be classified within true origins. The questions which arise from this are: (1) What is karma? and (2) What are delusions?

KARMA
Karma simply means action. Every action we do is karma.

Physical, Verbal and Mental Actions
Karma can be classified into three types of actions: those of body, of speech, and of mind. That is, karma can be divided into physical, mental and verbal action.

Virtuous, Non-Virtuous, and Neutral Actions
Karma can also be classified into three types according to the quality of the action as (a) virtuous, (b) non-virtuous, or (c) neutral actions.

(a) Virtuous actions are any actions the individual does for the benefit of self or others. (Benefit in this case means actual improvement. It does not include material gain at others' expense.) For example, by observing the rules of morality, one benefits both oneself and others.

(b) Non-virtuous actions are simply the opposite of virtuous ac-

tions. Doing things which adversely affect other people brings negative karmic results. Such actions are harmful both to oneself and to others. Obvious examples of non-virtuous actions include killing and stealing. Less obvious examples are wasting one's time when one should be studying, not engaging in other meaningful activities when the opportunity to do so exists, or not showing respect or wishing to repay those who have been kind to you.

(c) Neutral actions are those actions which do not have either any adverse or any beneficial effect for oneself or others. Ordinary actions, such as just walking or driving along the road with no particular motivation, are of no harm or benefit to anyone.

Three categories according to the method of expression of the action.	Three categories according to non-virtuous, neutral or virtuous quality of the action.		
	Non-Virtuous	Neutral	Virtuous
Physical			
Verbal			
Mental			

Figure 3.1. Karma: three categories of expression and three categories of virtue

A teacher, for example, is likely to be accumulating more virtuous actions than non-virtuous actions in the sense that what s/he is doing is bringing benefit to other people. An animal slaughterer, by contrast, is repeatedly planning to kill animals and then actually doing so.

Those who give advice based on experience of the proper way to do things are performing virtuous verbal actions. Such activity is beneficial to both the giver and the recipient of the advice. In contrast, lying and divisive talk, meant to separate people, cause harm to others and are therefore non-virtuous verbal actions.

Neutral verbal actions include most of the speech people engage in. It is not particularly aimed at improving or harming our own or other people's situations.

Virtuous mental actions include thinking about ways to improve oneself or society. *Neutral mental actions* include thinking about ordinary things, such as the thoughts one has while playing games and so forth.

Virtuous and non-virtuous actions can be further divided into ten categories each. These include three categories of physical actions, four of verbal actions, and three of mental actions for both virtuous and non-virtuous actions. The ten categories of non-virtuous and ten categories of virtuous actions are presented in Figure 3.2.

The ten non-virtuous actions include (a) three physical actions—killing, stealing and sexual misconduct; (b) four verbal actions—lying, divisive talk, using harsh words which cause other people distress, and engaging in idle gossip; and (c) three mental actions—thinking about one's objects of attachment, engaging in thoughts of harming others, and engaging in wrong views.

The non-virtuous physical actions and many of the non-virtuous verbal actions are self-explanatory. Examples of idle gossip include talking pointlessly about anything or talking about something which takes one away from virtuous purposeful activity. Examples of non-virtuous mental activities include thinking about one's objects of attachment, such as one's own wealth or another person's wealth, or engaging in the thought of harming others. Engaging in wrong views can occur by means of being led astray by other people who say there is no such thing as dharma or no benefit from practicing dharma.

The ten virtuous actions consist of abandoning or restraining from the ten non-virtuous actions. However, generally this is amplified to suggest an active development of positive actions contrary to and in place of the non-virtuous actions.

Virtuous physical actions include three types of actions:

(1) Abandoning killing means not just not to kill, but rather to do something to attempt to save lives. It also includes actions

Karma (Actions)	Non-Virtuous	Virtuous
Physical actions	1. Killing 2. Stealing 3. Sexual misconduct	1. Abandoning killing 2. Abandoning stealing 3. Abandoning sexual misconduct
Verbal actions	4. Lying 5. Divisive talk 6. Using harsh words 7. Idle gossip	4. Abandoning lying 5. Abandoning divisive talk 6. Abandoning harsh words 7. Abandoning idle gossip
Mental actions	8. Engaging the mind in objects of attachment 9. Engaging in thoughts of harming others 10. Wrong views	8. Abandoning the mind of attachment 9. Abandoning thoughts of harming others 10. Abandoning wrong views

Figure 3.2. Non-virtuous and virtuous physical, mental and verbal actions

intended to protect people and to help them improve their situations, or to live longer and better lives.

(2) Abandoning stealing again means more than simply stopping the action of stealing. Thinking about the problems, disputes and unhappiness caused by people taking others' possessions leads one to abandon stealing. It also results in the decision to do something positive in its place. One tries to generate happiness and satisfaction with one's own situation and tries not to generate the thought, "Oh, if only I had this!" Then one tries to share one's resources with others as much as possible in order to bring about some help to other beings as well.

(3) Abandoning sexual misconduct. Having observed the faults of sexual misconduct, such as being socially outcast oneself or causing emotional damage to self and others, one abandons those actions that are generally unacceptable in terms of law and general social values. One observes normal social mores and abandons those actions which contradict them. One attempts to generate minds (attitudes) which will prevent such action occurring in the future.

Virtuous verbal actions include the following four types of actions:

(4) Abandoning telling lies. One observes the faults of telling lies and abandons this behavior. One then focuses both on telling the truth and on saying things which will benefit others.

(5) Abandoning divisive talk. Having abandoned divisive talk, one tries to engage in actions which will enhance good relationships between people. For example, one may attempt to bring people together after they have had some disagreement or assist them to resolve an issue if they have never been in agreement.

(6) Abandoning harsh words. After one abandons using words which cause distress to others, then one engages in speech which is pleasurable for others to listen to. One attempts to say things which will cause happiness for others.

(7) Abandoning idle gossip. Seeing the time one wastes in idle gossip, one tries to always say things which have meaning.

Virtuous mental actions include three types of actions:

(8) Abandoning the mind of attachment. The antidote to the mind of attachment is to give up the faults of samsara. This results from having seen the faults of engaging in a desirous mind.

(9) Abandoning thoughts of harming others. After one abandons thoughts of harming others, one attempts to engage in thoughts of compassion and love for other beings.

(10) Abandoning wrong views. One attempts to generate an accurate understanding of the correct view. This is done in terms of dharma as well as in understanding what is appropriate in society. One studies dharma in order to create a proper understand-

ing of the teachings, and one also attempts to respect the rules of society.

In summary, these ten non-virtuous and ten virtuous actions have been explained very briefly from the perspective of karma (actions). Non-virtuous actions cause us to be in samsara, whereas the virtuous actions serve as the antidote to these actions and their effects.

DELUSION

The root of delusion is ignorance. Ignorance is a mind which apprehends something which is not in accord with reality. That is, it apprehends something which does not fit with the reality of the situation. All other delusions can be traced back to ignorance.

Dullness of the mind is another type of ignorance. It is a dullness or darkness of the mind, in which, although the actual situation is perceived accurately, it is not perceived clearly. The dull mind is not clear enough or sharp enough to perceive the object as it really is.

Just as there are both gross and subtle aspects of any phenomenon apprehended by the mind, so there are gross (ignorance) and subtle (dullness) aspects of delusion to the mind(s) of the person apprehending the situation. All of the delusions can be traced back to ignorance. The basic delusions of attachment and aversion are based in ignorance. A whole array of specific other delusions arise from attachment and aversion.

The six root delusions are traditionally presented in two categories. The first five root delusions are considered as one category—the five delusions which are not views. The sixth root delusion (deluded view) and its divisions (the five delusions which are views) are considered as the second category. When Buddha said "These are the Arya's true source of suffering," he was referring to ignorance and delusion.[1]

The Five Root Delusions Which Are Not Views

The delusions in this category arise through familiarity but not from dogma or wrong reasons.

THE SIX ROOT DELUSIONS

1. Ignorance of cause and effect
2. Aversion/ Hatred
3. Attachment/ Desire
4. Pride
5. Deluded doubt

THE FIVE WHICH ARE NOT VIEWS

6. Deluded view: the result of ignorance and attachment

    a. View of the transitory collection
    b. Extreme view
        (1) past
        (2) future
    c. Wrong view of the ten non-virtuous actions
    d. Grasping at one's view as supreme
    e. Wrong view of behavior

THE FIVE WHICH ARE VIEWS

Figure 3.3. The six root delusions

(1) Ignorance is a deluded mind which obscures the mind from apprehending the nature of the object clearly.

(2) Aversion/Hatred is a deluded mind which feels strong aversion toward others or self.

(3) Attachment/Desire is a deluded mind which feels strong attraction towards self, others or phenomena.

(4) Pride is a deluded mind which views oneself as unreasonably high and which looks down on others.

(5) Deluded doubt refers to a doubt which causes one to develop negative emotions. For example, when someone develops doubt toward the law of cause and effect, then due to such doubt s/he generates negative emotions. Such a doubt is known as deluded doubt.

The Five Delusions Which Are Views

(6) Deluded view. A person adopts a certain view due to ignorance and attachment. These become mixed, which results in an erroneous assessment of the situation. There are five of these deluded views.

(a) View of the transitory collection[2] is basically a mistaken view of the self. One views what is there and comes to view this as an independent, unchanging phenomenon. (That is, one believes one's self to be inherently existent, or as existing from its own side.)

(b) Extreme view. There are two types of extreme views, divided according to time (past and future).

(1) Past. The extreme view of the past holds that there is no such thing as past lives.

(2) Future. This view holds that there is no such thing as future lives, or that there is no hope for liberation or omniscience.

(c) Wrong view of the ten non-virtuous actions. The ten non-virtuous actions were presented above. The last of these is holding wrong views, and has been explained.

(d) Grasping at one's false view as supreme is the wrong view which holds one's own false idea to be the only correct view. It refers to views that are not completely correct. For example, a scientist may have his own idea of the way the universe began and say, "This is my idea, and it is the only correct theory that there is." In essence, this is both the delusion which thinks one's own idea is correct and the quality of mind which grasps onto the idea that it is the only correct view.

(e) Wrong view of behavior or ethical conduct refers to views of extreme ascetic practices which have no adequate logical foundation. For example, some non-Buddhist practitioners go around naked or torture their bodies. In addition, they hold tightly to their view of ascetic behaviors as the supreme one and also take pride in themselves for their ability to practice such behaviors. There is no rational foundation for the specific practices. Often the only explanation that can be given is a specific tradition or teaching. Similarly, people often adopt certain attitudes about

foods to eat or to avoid, based solely on cultural preferences, with no basis in reason. They then hold onto their view of this behavior as the best type of behavior to practice.

TRUE ORIGINS OF SUFFERING AS THE CAUSE OF TRUE SUFFERING

The Second Noble Truth, the true origins of suffering, is the cause of the First Noble Truth, true suffering. This statement describes the ways in which the causes of suffering, ignorance and delusion, give rise to the effect, true suffering. The Second Noble Truth refers to karmic action and afflictive emotions as the cause of suffering. Ignorance and delusion are the cause of afflictive emotions (see Figure 3.4).

IGNORANCE	AFFLICTIVE EMOTIONS	KARMIC ACTION	TRUE SUFFERING
of the selflessness of persons and phenomena ➡	attachment aversion	➡ physical mental verbal	➡ suffering

Figure 3.4. True origins of suffering as the cause of true suffering

The law of cause and effect deals with specific actions and their results. In terms of the first two Noble Truths, which concern suffering, the actions to be addressed are negative actions, because suffering is their effect.

For example, the animal slaughterer engages in the act of killing. He would not do so if he were fully aware of the effects of his action. Basically, his actions can be traced back to his ignorance. It is his ignorance which is the real cause of the situation. Through misunderstanding the situation, he generates attachment to taking life and those things (meat, profit) he perceives as benefits from doing so. His action is indirectly motivated by ignorance and directly motivated by attachment. However, it is ignorance which serves as the basis for his attachment. Without it, neither the delusion of attachment nor the action of killing the animal could occur.

Even if the slaughterer is killing only for meat for himself, the cause is ignorance, which results in a wrong view of himself. From this, he develops attachment to the meat that will result from killing the animal. As a result, he engages in the act of killing and has accumulated the karma of killing. The causal sequence begins with ignorance. A wrong view of self develops out of this basic ignorance of cause and effect. The wrong view of the self serves as the basis for attachment to self, and consequently in attachment to killing in order to preserve that self.

EFFECTS OF ACTIONS (KARMA)

There are three types of effects which arise from a strong action, such as killing. These are: (1) the fully ripening effect, (2) the effect similar to the cause, and (3) the environmental effect.

All three effects result from any strong action, but vary according to the level of severity of that action. The level of severity of the action depends on factors such as the object of the action and the motivation for engaging in it. These factors determine the seriousness of the action, or the strength of its three effects.

The fully ripening effect of the most serious form of killing is rebirth in a hell realm. The fully ripening effect of a less serious form of killing is rebirth as an animal, and the fully ripening effect of the least serious form is rebirth as a human.

The least serious form of an action does not serve as the main cause which propels a person into their next life. Rather, the fully ripening effect is experienced in terms of problems they face within the next life. For example, the result of the least serious form of killing is that one will have a short life span in the next life.

The effect similar to the cause for the least serious form of killing is that the person takes pleasure in the act of killing in future lives. The force of the prior action maintains its influence over the aggregates.

The environmental effect of the least negatively forceful form of the act of killing consists of the presence of many persons who cause the individual harm. Inanimate objects in the environment also present threats to the person's health or life. The amount of harm actually done by persons or objects in the environment varies.

Actions related to strong attachment to wealth or possessions provide another example of the levels of cause and effect of action. As with the example of killing, ignorance is the root of the attachment which leads to actions of miserliness. Many repeated actions of miserliness are necessary to produce an effect of similar force to that of a single act of killing. A great deal of the mind of attachment must be accumulated in order to constitute the most serious level of action, in contrast to the mind which produces the strong direct action of a single act of killing.

The effects of actions can also be illustrated by the example of repeated actions of miserliness.

The most serious form of the *fully ripening effect* of repeated actions of miserliness is rebirth in a ghost-like realm of hungry spirits. The fully ripening effect of the middling level of seriousness is rebirth as an animal, particularly a type of animal who has difficulty in finding food, drink and shelter. The fully ripening effect of the least strong level of this cause is rebirth as a human who experiences the effects of this action during this lifetime. The individual remains under the influence of others and experiences powerlessness, lack of freedom and lack of resources during their lifetime.

The effect similar to the cause for these persons is the continued influence of a strong mind of attachment, the inability to find satisfaction with what they have, and continuous striving to achieve more.

The environmental effect of miserliness is that, in one's efforts to improve one's situation, one experiences a lack of help from others as well as obstacles to achieving these goals from inanimate objects.

FOUR CHARACTERISTICS OF FULL KARMA
There are four characteristics which are necessary for a complete action. A complete action is necessary for the full effect(s) of that

1. Action of killing

CAUSE	EFFECT		
Seriousness of Action	Fully Ripening Effect	Effect Similar to Cause	Environmental Effect
Most Serious	Rebirth in a hell realm		
Middling Level	Rebirth as an animal		
Least Serious	Rebirth as a human with short life span	Liking for the act of killing	Many external obstacles to maintaining life, health; many enemies

2. Actions stemming from Miserliness

CAUSE	EFFECT		
Seriousness	Fully Ripening Effect	Effect Similar to Cause	Environmental Effect
A. Most Serious	Rebirth as a hungry spirit		
B. Middling Level	Rebirth as an animal with problems finding food and shelter		
C. Least Serious	Rebirth as a human with lack of resources, powerless	Attachments to wealth, objects. Lack of satisfaction with what one has.	External obstacles to finding wealth or other objects of attachment.

Figure 3.5. Examples of cause and effect of actions

action (karma) to occur. These characteristics represent different phases of any action. They are: (1) intention, (2) preparation, (3) performance, and (4) finality (rejoicing).

In most instances, not all of these phases of action are present. Therefore, some but not all of the karma is accumulated. That is, the strength of the karma accumulated varies with the completeness of the action. A person may perform a negative action (such as lying) from a good intention (to avoid causing distress) and therefore the full karma is not accumulated. Similarly, there may be both positive and negative aspects within one phase of action, such as occurs when one acts out of a mixed motive. In the case of the slaughterer, for example, the intention of making a profit may be mixed with some motivation to help the community.

Karma can be accumulated on both the individual level and the group level. For example, when Indira Gandhi, the prime minister of India, was murdered, there were only one or two people who actually performed the action. However, many people met and discussed what was to be done beforehand. There were many people involved in the intention to kill her, and in making the preparations to do so. Few people, however, were involved in actually performing the action. Those persons who contributed financial or other assistance to the action did participate indirectly in the actual performance of the action. Finally, all those persons who were glad that the murder had occurred accumulated the karma associated with the finality of the action.

Those who participated in all four phases of the action accumulated the full karma of killing a person. On the other hand, someone who had the intention and took part in the planning but dropped out (for any reason) before contributing to the actual murder, did not accumulate the full karma. Similarly, all those who were glad to hear the news that the prime minister had been killed, but who had had no intention to kill her, nor contributed to planning or carrying out that action, accumulated some but not all of the karma of killing. Those persons who took part in all four phases of the complete action will experience its results in the form of a fully ripening effect.

POSITIVE AND NEGATIVE ACTIONS

Actions (karma) can also be classified as positive, negative or mixed actions. (Traditionally, these categories have been termed white, black and mixed actions).

The direction and strength of the force of action accumulated also varies with the type and consistency of the quality of all phases of that action. All phases of positive actions are virtuous. All phases of negative actions are non-virtuous.

Mixed actions include both virtuous and non-virtuous aspects, either as different phases or within one or more of the phases of a complete action. For example, a good intention may produce a bad action. The intention of stopping a murderer from killing someone may result in the action of killing the murderer. The person who killed the murderer may regret his/her action. Different phases of the same action may be either virtuous or non-virtuous.

The effects of mixed action are experienced in mixed results. The karma experienced will include both suffering and happiness. Also, the quality of the action may be mixed within any one or more of the phases of action. For example, the slaughterer may intend to kill animals both for the profit and for the benefit of the community, so the intention is mixed. However, the action of killing is always a negative action.

On the group level, if a nation of people were undergoing some problem, and they were all engaged in thinking about the problem, planning ways to solve it, and taking action to remedy it, and rejoicing in the success of their efforts, then the effect of that action is a positive effect.

PROPELLING AND COMPLETING KARMA

Karma can also be considered from the point of view of its division into the two categories of propelling (throwing) and completing karma. Propelling karma is that which propels one into a particular form of rebirth. Completing karma brings about the experiences within that life. They too, may be congruent or incongruent with regard to being virtuous (positive) or non-virtuous (negative) in character.

Propelling karma throws one into rebirth in a particular realm. If the propelling karma results from negative action, one is born in one of the three lower realms of animals, hungry spirits or hell beings. If it is the result of positive action, rebirth occurs in one of the three higher realms of humans, gods or demi-gods.

Completing karma brings about the experiences one has within a given lifetime. It brings an end to the karma that propelled a being into a particular life. It is called completing karma because the experiences brought about by completing karma gradually bring an end to a specific rebirth.

As stated above, propelling and completing karma may be of different kinds. Positive propelling karma may lead a person to rebirth as a human in circumstances of wealth. Negative completing karma may bring about difficulties with finances or possessions. Negative propelling karma may result in rebirth as an animal. Positive completing karma brings pleasurable experiences to that animal.

SUMMARY OF KARMA

Karma can be classified in terms of (1) its effects—as fully ripening, similar to the cause, or environmental effects; (2) the completeness of the action; (3) the type and consistency of the action (positive, negative and mixed) or (4) the results (propelling or completing karma) of the action.

Complete actions include all phases of action (intention, planning, carrying out the action, and rejoicing in the results). Incomplete actions lack one or more of these phases.

Positive (white) actions are complete, virtuous actions. Negative (black) actions are complete non-virtuous actions. Mixed actions occur when some phases of a complete action are virtuous, while other phases are non-virtuous in character. Mixed actions also include those in which any one phase has both virtuous and non-virtuous qualities.

Propelling karma throws one into a particular form of rebirth. Completing karma results in the experiences within that rebirth, and gradually brings about the end of that particular lifetime.

Interactions between these various characteristics of karma result in a wide variety of possible combinations of fully ripening effects, effects similar to the cause and environmental effects of positive, negative or mixed karma which may be complete or incomplete and determine the form of rebirth and the experiences one has within that rebirth.

4 How True Origins Give Rise to True Suffering

TRUE ORIGINS AND TRUE SUFFERING

True origins give rise to true suffering, which in turn gives rise to true origins. The relationship is like that of the proverbial chicken and egg.

In any particular instance, one can identify a specific causal sequence. One person becomes angry and strikes another. Delusion causes a negative action. The person struck becomes angry and strikes back. Again, delusion results in a negative action, delusion coming before anger in both instances.

In broader terms, although delusion must occur before a negative action results from it as above, it is also true that negative actions cause delusion to increase. The performance of negative actions results in negative karma which further increases one's delusions. These, in turn, result in further negative actions in a vicious cycle of delusion and negative action.

True origins give rise to true suffering, and true suffering gives rise to true origins in an endless cycle termed samsara. *Samsara* simply means to circle, and is often translated as cyclic existence. There is no apparent means to break this cycle.

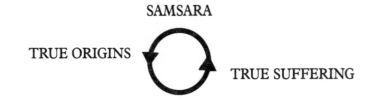

Figure 4.1: Samsara: the relationship between true origins and true suffering

One is caught in the cycle of samsara. One performs both virtuous and non-virtuous actions, and therefore experiences a variety of different states of existence. However, even in the hell realms, the lowest form of rebirth, once the karma that propelled one to that state has been exhausted, another action will ripen, perhaps resulting in a higher rebirth. True origins propel one from one rebirth to another. True sufferings are experienced within that rebirth. One is trapped, going from one state to another.

THE TWELVE LINKS OF DEPENDENT ORIGINATION

The twelve links of dependent origination provide the explanation of how ignorance, actions and suffering, and the cycle of compulsive rebirth (samsara) interact to create or continue suffering from one lifetime to the next.

The twelve links of dependent arising are presented according to their temporal order of causality. The causal links produce the bases of suffering (name and form, the six sense spheres, physical sense consciousness and feeling) and result in the actual sufferings of birth, aging and death.[1]

As shown in Figure 4.2, ignorance and compounded karma are the first two links of the twelve links of dependent origination.

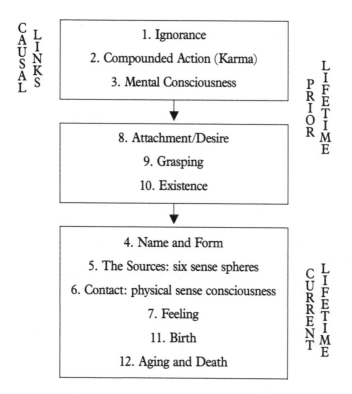

CAUSAL LINKS

PRIOR LIFETIME

1. Ignorance

2. Compounded Action (Karma)

3. Mental Consciousness

8. Attachment/Desire

9. Grasping

10. Existence

CURRENT LIFETIME

4. Name and Form

5. The Sources: six sense spheres

6. Contact: physical sense consciousness

7. Feeling

11. Birth

12. Aging and Death

Figure 4.2. The twelve links of dependent origination: causal
sequence

CAUSAL LINKS OF THE PRIOR LIFETIME

The causal links of the previous lifetime propel beings into the
conditions of their current rebirth. They include ignorance, action, mental consciousness and the attachments which result
from them.

Ignorance

The first link is ignorance. A person who abandons the act of
killing will be used as an example to help in the understanding
of the twelve links. Even someone who engages in the virtuous

action of abandoning killing has the first type of ignorance, that is, the ignorance as to the true (ultimate) nature of phenomena. This person still has the ignorance of the ultimate nature of phenomena and grasps at self and phenomena as being truly or inherently existent.

Suppose a person with this ignorance engaged in the act of abandoning killing, and decided, "I'm not going to engage in killing beings anymore." At that time, with that particular action, they accumulated a certain karma.

Karma

Karma is the second link. It is explained in terms of the analogy of planting seeds in a field to grow a particular crop. In order for the sprouts to appear, a seed must be there in the first place. However, just the seed alone is not sufficient. Certain conditions are needed for the seed to sprout. Moisture is obviously an essential condition. Without moisture, the seed would never give rise to any sprout.

Mental Consciousness

The seed in the example given above is similar to the act, the particular karma, of abandoning killing. The field in which it is planted, or the place where this particular karma abides, is the mental consciousness. The seed is like the actual action (the karma) of abandoning killing, and the consciousness is like a field in which the seed is planted. This mind, that is, mental consciousness, is therefore the third of these twelve links. The first link is ignorance, the second is compounded karma, and the third is mental consciousness.

These first three links constitute the projecting branches of the causal sequence of the twelve links of dependent arising. They are also the first three links of dependent arising arranged according to temporal sequence. They are created in a lifetime prior to the current life.

Desirous Attachment

Desirous attachment (craving) is like the moisture which helps the karma to bear fruit, that is, to bring about an effect. Without this strong emotion of desirous attachment or craving toward cyclic existence (samsara) in one's mind, this particular karma (action) will not give rise to a real effect. Desirous attachment is the eighth of the twelve links.

Grasping
Grasping is the ninth link. It is also like the moisture which acts as a condition for propelling karma to manifest. It is very much like desirous attachment (the eighth link) but is much stronger. For example, when we see a beautiful flower, we develop craving for it. The initial craving for the flower is the craving referred to in the eighth link. When such craving becomes stronger and we feel like grasping the flower and possessing it, then it is the grasping referred to in the ninth link.

When a person dies, or is on the verge of real death, the gross physical consciousness, that is, the gross physical senses such as the body sense, are lost as they gradually subside into the mental consciousness. So the person cannot see gross forms. S/he cannot feel things with her/his body. But still the mental consciousness is present. The person is in something like a dream state. Certain forms of attachment come into the mind. S/he may wish for certain things or to go to certain places. Various forms appear to this mental consciousness. These are said to indicate where this person is going to be reborn.

If the person is going to be reborn as an animal, there will be appearances related to the animal realm. If s/he is going to be reborn as a human, then there will be certain human forms and so forth appearing to the mind and attachment toward the abodes and places where humans live. If s/he is going to be reborn as a deity, there will be appearances to the mental consciousness related to what rebirth in a god realm would bring about. This is the same for any particular birth s/he would take. The appearances reflect where the person will be born. These appearances arise when the person is on the verge of dying, after the gross physical consciousness or physical senses have ceased and just the mental consciousness remains. This process is said to be the ninth link, which is adopting or taking on, and refers to taking on a new rebirth, a new life.

Existence

Existence is the tenth link. When the strongest propelling karmic imprint arises during the time of death, the dying person will have a vision according to that karmic imprint where s/he is going to be reborn. When such a vision arises, the person develops craving and grasping for it, and that becomes the condition for that particular karmic imprint to manifest.[2]

So now we've explained six of the twelve links. These links must necessarily be present, arise, before the person dies. They occur in one particular lifetime before a person dies. They are called the causal links.

At the point when the effect of a particular action comes to fruition, the relationship ceases between the body and mind of the particular life which is coming to an end. The consciousness departs from the body. This is the point where the person's consciousness and body of one particular life end their relationship. Now the mind, the consciousness, will be reborn in a new form. This is the eleventh link, which is known as birth.

Birth/Existence

There is an intermediate period (bardo) between the end of one life and the start of another, however. For example, if a being is going to be reborn as a human, that being will have a subtle body similar to the one which s/he will adopt at the time of her or his new birth.

This form is a very subtle form. It's not made up of gross matter, so it's not hindered by gross matter. It can go anywhere. It's not something you can see with the naked eye. The eleventh link occurs when the person takes rebirth in the actual form. Although the bardo being[3] is a form, it's not the actual human form. The actual human form is said to be the eleventh link, birth.

For example, if we listen to a radio station which is being broadcast from Delhi, there has to be some sort of signal which travels between Delhi and the place where we're listening to the radio, such as Dharamsala. However, it's not the actual sound which travels. The thing which is going between Delhi and Dharamsala is the ability to produce the sound. It's not the sound itself. When radio waves traveling between two points such as Delhi and Dharamsala reach a receiver, they will then produce the effect of a sound similar to the one which was initially produced in Delhi.

The actual sound is similar to the consciousness, the third of the twelve links. The force which causes the radio waves to go from one place to another in our illustration is like karma, the second of the twelve links. When the consciousness is propelled by the karma to a certain place, then one takes birth. In a similar way, the sound waves go from one place to another, and having reached a certain destination and a receiver, then the various sounds come forth. This is similar to the way that one takes birth. A particular karmic force propels a consciousness to one place and then one is reborn in a specific form.

CAUSAL LINKS OF THE CURRENT LIFETIME
The causal links of the previous lifetime are completed in the current lifetime. This occurs from prenatal development through aging and death.

Name and Form
When the consciousness arrives in a certain place, it enters into the womb of the mother. It is said to enter into a space between the point where the sperm and the ovum meet. It becomes surrounded by the mixture of the sperm and the egg of the mother. At this point, the fourth of these links, the link of name and form, is complete. That is, the link of name and form is completed when the consciousness enters into relationship with the physical elements which will produce a body.

The Sources
The next link (the fifth link) is called the sources. At this stage the mental consciousness itself becomes slightly grosser. The

very subtle form of consciousness which actually entered the womb becomes slightly grosser at this stage. However, there are still no manifest consciousnesses such as the eye consciousness or physical sense consciousness and so forth.

Contact and Form

Gradually the sense consciousness will begin to appear. When the physical consciousness appears, then the sixth link of contact is completed. Even though there is a physical sense consciousness, it is not a particularly clear one at this stage. For example, if one was to rub some rough or smooth objects against this form, the sense consciousness would not be sufficiently powerful to feel them. However, with the process of time, this physical sense consciousness becomes more and more gross, and eventually it is able to experience heat and cold and so forth. At this stage, the seventh link, the link of feeling, is complete. For example, all of us present here are said to be at this seventh stage of feeling.

Aging and Death

There are two parts to the final, twelfth link, aging and death. Although we have yet to enter into death in this particular lifetime, we are actively engaged in the process of aging. Aging is the process of coming ever closer to the time of death. Death occurs when the life of a particular person cannot continue any longer and there's no way that the person can be revived. At this point, the second part of this final link of death is completed.

Again, there are two aspects to death: death and having died. At the stage of death one reaches the point where life can no longer be prolonged. Having died is the stage where the consciousness has completely separated from the body. All the gross consciousnesses have subsided or dissolved into the subtle consciousness and only the subtle consciousness is left. This subtle consciousness has separated from the body (the physical form) and is heading towards the new life. This is the state of having died. The twelfth link is completely finished.

In terms of our own completion of the twelve links, our former

life, the life prior to this one, created the first three links of ignorance, action or karma, and consciousness. The eight, ninth
and tenth links—craving, grasping and existence—were also
completed by the lifetime prior to the present one.

The remaining six links are to be completed by this present
life. In fact, five of these six are already finished, and it is only
the final link, that of death, which is not completed yet. However, at this present stage we are accumulating many different
types of karma which may well give rise to any birth, be it in a
human, animal or any other realm. We are engaged in those actions that can bring about such results in the future.

SUMMARY OF THE TWELVE LINKS

In summary, in terms of the twelve links as they relate to us, six
were completed by ourselves in a prior lifetime. We are now engaged in completing the six which will see completion in a future life. The first six links were completed in a former life. Six
links are completed in this life. So that is the whole series. Those
two lives are the series of twelve links. However, we will create
six links in this life which will be completed in a future life, and
that again, is another set of twelve links.

If, for example, one is engaged in a particular job, such as
teaching, then one is presently enjoying the wages from this form
of good work. In dependence upon the wages one receives, one
can buy various things and so forth. Also one is engaged in actions in the work which will give rise to, lead to, gaining wages
next month. So there are these two different aspects.

At any one time, there is this cause and effect relationship going on. We can't point a finger and say "This is the start of the
process." This whole cyclic process, first creating six links in this
lifetime, then completing six links in the next life, is what is referred to by the term samsara. Samsara means cyclic existence.
The cycle is the continuous creating of karma and being reborn.

The ripening of many past actions results in the experience
of suffering. The aggregates of body and mind serve as the basis for our experience of that suffering. The aggregates possess
the nature of suffering.

THE ENVIRONMENT

The environment is also said to be true suffering, that is, to have the nature of suffering. Suffering naturally arises from the aggregates and from the environment. As the nature of water is to flow downhill, and the nature of fire is to burn, so the nature of the aggregates and of the environment is to produce suffering. It is not likely that either fire or water will change; that water will burn or fire will make things moist. It is characteristic of those things to bring about their respective effects.

In the same way, within samsara, attachment cannot bring genuine happiness, it can only bring suffering. The stronger the attachment, the stronger the suffering. One might take any particular object in the environment and think, ''If I were to become more attached to that, what would the effect of that be?'' The only effect could be that just as much as one increases one's attachment to the object, the suffering one would have to experience would have to increase to the same extent. The environment is termed true suffering because suffering naturally results if one generates delusions and the consequent aversion and/or attachment to objects in that environment.

The body is the real form of true suffering. All our experience is basically in dependence upon having this form. On the gross level, birth, aging, sickness and death are all experiences of suffering. The body experiences a great deal of physical suffering during the birth process. Aging begins immediately after birth, so we are continuously moving toward a state of degeneration. During our lifetime, we are continuously faced with illness, disease and various types of physical problems. Finally, there is death, which no one can escape.

FOUR CHARACTERISTICS OF TRUE SUFFERING

The true origins of karma and the true origins of delusion give rise to the first of the truths, that of true suffering. There are both general and specific characteristics of true suffering. Both address the nature of true suffering.

There are four general characteristics of true suffering. These are (1) impermanence, (2) suffering, (3) emptiness, and (4) self-lessness.

IMPERMANENCE

The physical and mental aggregates have a changeable nature and are therefore impermanent.[4] Impermanence includes two categories, gross and subtle impermanence. Gross impermanence is the impermanence which can be observed with the passage of time. Subtle impermanence is momentary impermanence. It cannot generally be observed and must be supported by logic.

Gross Impermanence

Gross impermanence describes the gross changes all compounded phenomena undergo with the passage of noticeable amounts of time. In terms of the largest amount of time we can generally think of, the changes in the continents, oceans, mountain ranges and river beds reflect the gross impermanence of our planet. In more modern terms, the changes in the growth of cities over decades and years reflect their gross impermanence. As time passes, transformations occur. We see changes in the physical growth of an infant or child in just weeks, months or years. Time passes and things necessarily undergo change. The changes we can see are manifestations of gross impermanence.

In any situation, the people who are present at any one time, the objects they are using, and the society they live in are all in a state of constant transformation. Some are improving, while others are going through stages of degeneration. It is said that in this era, the world in general is in a state of degeneration. Although specific phenomena or situations may be in a state of improvement, the actual causes and conditions to bring about improvement are less common now than in the past. The causes and conditions of deterioration are both stronger and greater in number than those which cause improvement.

Many perceivable changes occur during the space of a month. One eats and sleeps and engages in many different activities during that time. Likewise, within the course of a single day, there are many changes in what we experience. The things we come in contact with are all in the process of change. If we do not consider the fact that things are in a constant state of change, then what naturally comes to mind is a fixed picture of the process of reality.

For example, if we stood outside on a sunny day and saw a shadow caused by the sun, then turned our heads and looked at something else for a moment, when we turned back, the shadow would have moved. However, we might not notice it, unless we put marks where the shadow was in the first place. Even though we know time is progressing, and the shadow is moving, still, a static picture of reality is what comes to our mind.

If we sat still and stared at the shadow, it might not appear to our eyes that is was actually moving. The shadows caused by a mountain are in one direction at sunrise and an entirely different direction by the time the sun sets. We can see a great change has occurred due to the sun's movements and our movements in relation to the sun. However, if we had just sat staring at the shadows, we wouldn't necessarily get that impression.

The changes resulting from the impermanence which is due to the progression of time are present even within short spaces of time, such as an hour and so forth. Gross impermanence is obvious, and can be observed directly. Therefore it does not need any logical reasoning to prove that it occurs.

Subtle Impermanence

Subtle impermanence refers to those changes which occur in such short spaces of time that they cannot be observed. The changes that occur within seconds, tenths of seconds and hundredths of seconds or less are classified as subtle impermanence. They require logical reasoning for proof of their existence.

As the second hand which goes around the sixty marks on a clock marks the passage of one minute, so the establishment of a minute is based on the passage of seconds. Again, as the minute hand going around the clock one time marks the passage of an hour, so hours are established due to the passage of minutes.

Then as the hours go to form days, so days are established in dependence upon the passage of hours. These are examples of gross impermanence.

The changes which go on within short spaces of time, such as seconds and parts of seconds, are classified as subtle impermanence. For example, we can notice how a table changes from year to year. That is gross impermanence. The changes which the table undergoes within the spaces of minutes and seconds are not things which we can notice. These changes represent subtle impermanence.

All products (all contaminated compounded phenomena) undergo both gross and subtle forms of impermanence. Although some improvement may occur in samsaric phenomena when they first begin, in general they are in a state of disintegration and deterioration. In the state of buddhahood, however, although both gross and subtle forms of change occur, the process of change does not lead to any form of degeneration. One reaches a stable level, still marked by the process of change but without deterioration.

Beings on the levels leading up to buddhahood are in a state of improvement. As normal human beings however, there are stages of improvement and increase, and stages of deterioration. This is true of the environment, the objects within the environment and of the beings themselves.

There are no samsaric beings who stay in a constant state of happiness. Pleasure and displeasure, happiness and suffering occur in a serial process.

By analogy, water generally flows downward; that is its nature. In special cases, it can be made to flow uphill by the use of machines and so forth. However, even in these instances, there are limits which cannot be exceeded. The water has to stay within those limits or go downward. Likewise, no worthwhile form of improvement comes about naturally. We have to strive to attain it. The more worthwhile it is, the more effort is required. On the other hand, deterioration or degeneration requires no effort. It occurs naturally.

Gross changes are gross impermanence, subtle changes are

subtle impermanence. Any changes that occur within the space of a year depend upon the changes that occurred within the space of a month. The changes in a month depend upon the changes that occurred within the weeks of that month, and so forth, right down to the dependence of the changes within seconds upon those within fractions of seconds.

The motion of water in a river provides an example of the appearance of momentary change. A ripple forms, then another ripple, and the process seems momentarily similar. However, a continuous process of change is occurring. In the same way, in any particular object, the object may have the same aspect from moment to moment, and the momentary changes are very difficult to notice. One does not see the motion of a river from an airplane. Rather, one notices only the pattern of the waves and eddies. It is not until one gets closer to the river that the flowing process of the water can be seen. The subtle changes of one moment produce something very similar to themselves in the next moment, and therefore are very difficult to notice.

Similarly, if a light is twirled in a circle fast enough, the eye does not see the motion, but only the circle of light. Similarly, we see phenomena as constant things without seeing the subtle process of continuous change which occurs. Therefore, we grasp at things as static phenomena, clinging to the notion of their stability and permanence. On this basis, we develop attachment and aversion to persons and things. Similarly, we hold on to the mind of attachment or aversion. We cling to the mind of anger based on a word or deed of some person at some past point in time.

The more we can get rid of grasping at things as being static, and the more we can think about the impermanent nature of things, the more we will be able to open our minds to achieving beneficial things in the long run. One's mind will turn more toward practicing virtuous actions and abandoning non-virtuous actions. Decreasing attachment to things as static also reduces the attachment to this life. With that, all of the worries associated with attachments are reduced, and the mind becomes more free.

Impermanence is a characteristic of all forms of suffering.

Suffering is based on causes and conditions, in a causal sequence. The most basic of theses causes is ignorance, misunderstanding the nature of phenomena. This ignorance leads to delusion. Delusion leads directly or indirectly to actions. All of the (worldly) phenomena tend to fall back into a state of degeneration. That is, they are constantly in a state of decrease.

SUFFERING
The second characteristic of true suffering is suffering. Ignorance is the basic cause of the actions which produce suffering. Karma and delusion act as the conditions for bringing about the actions which cause suffering.

No matter how hard one strives to satisfy one's desires, one's situation remains unsatisfactory. Things necessarily will fall into one of the following three categories.

(1) *Suffering of suffering:* one meets with things which actually cause harm.

(2) *Suffering of change:* one meets with things which, once attained, eventually lead one to generate regret at having come to meet them.

(3) *All-pervasive suffering:* this suffering is the effect of the causes and conditions for the five aggregates, which are the medium of our present suffering and the cause of our future suffering.

Buddha stated that all contaminated phenomena are suffering. The question that arises from this statement is, "Is the one who has the experience of suffering a phenomenon which is something different from the nature of suffering, or something which is in the nature of suffering?"

In many schools of Hindu thought, the self is considered to be something other than the contaminated aggregates. The body and mind are seen as being in a constant state of transformation, whereas the self is considered to be permanent and unchanging. Therefore, the aggregates of body and mind and the self are considered to be different entities without a strong relationship between them. The self is considered to be like a lion in a forest of aggregates. The lion abides within that forest, but is not the same as the forest.

The Buddhist schools, on the other hand, do not accept the existence of a self, I, or person which is separate from the aggregates. If the person were separate from the aggregates, and the nature of the person was unchanging, there would be no escape from suffering or samsara for that person. Many Buddhist texts do use terminology that suggests a self which is other than the aggregates (a person and his/her aggregates). Although this is not accepted from a philosophical point of view, it is consistent with the way that the self and the aggregates usually appear to the mind, and therefore it is often presented in this way.

It is important to understand what one is trying to refute in attempting to eliminate the wrong view of the self. A person who is completely separate from the body and mind (the aggregates) does not exist. What does exist is a person who is the same entity as the aggregates, the same undifferentiable entity as the aggregates.

EMPTINESS

Emptiness refers to the lack of there being a person who is completely identical with or separate from their body and mind (the aggregates). The self and the aggregates exist as a single entity. One grasps at the self as something different from the aggregates, but this is not the case. The idea of one's body or one's self as clean or pure is an example of a gross form of clinging to the notion of a solid, independently existing self, and can be seen in the many efforts to keep one's self and one's environment clean. According to Sutra, all of the contaminated aggregates are by nature unclean. If the aggregates are impure, and the self is not an entity separate from the aggregates, then the self is necessarily also impure. The person is of an impure nature.

"Contaminated aggregates" is the term used for the body and mind which are produced by karma and delusion. Although the person can be said to be different from the aggregates, the person is not a different entity from the aggregates. (The Tathagata essence is not talked about in terms of being pure or impure. It is something which is permanent. It is not caused by delusion and so forth. It is not affected by conditions or delusions or karma.)

SELFLESSNESS

Even though one has refuted the misconception that the self is completely different from the aggregates and one understands that self and aggregates are the same entity, the misconception that there is a self-supporting 'I' that establishes itself may still persist. Refutation of the existence of such a self-supporting 'I' is the characteristic of selflessness.

The belief that there is a real self-supporting, substantially existent self or person acts as the basis from which many delusions arise. The lower Buddhist tenet systems recognize this as the root of samsara. However, the Prasangikas, the highest school, say that the cause of samsara is a more subtle wrong view. This is the wrong view that the self and phenomena are established, or existent, from their own side.

THE FOUR SEALS

The Four Seals are the main points which differentiate Buddhist tenets from those of other systems of thought. The first three of the Four Seals address the four characteristics of true suffering. Realization of these four attributes of suffering counters our usual misconceptions about what constitutes happiness and suffering.[5]

All of the philosophical traditions within Buddhism explain the Four Truths within the context of the four characteristics of true suffering. They all explain how the true origins of delusion and karma give rise to true suffering, and then how, if one practices true paths, one can be led to the state of true cessations. The final characteristic which distinguishes Buddhism from other philosophical schools is contained in the phrase "Nirvana is peace." The Four Seals are stated in the following way:

1) All compounded phenomena are impermanent.
2) All contaminated phenomena are in the nature of suffering.
3) All phenomena are empty and selfless.
4) Nirvana is peace.

All Buddhist teachings can be condensed into these four points. Similarly, the bases, the paths and the results of Buddhism can be found within these four points. These four points are seen as the root of Buddhism.

ALL COMPOUNDED PHENOMENA ARE IMPERMANENT

Even though all compounded phenomena are in a constant state of transformation, samsaric beings grasp at them as having a permanent, static nature. The processes of gross and subtle changes are not recognized. Delusions, such as attachment, are created through the power of grasping after permanence. These attachments generate actions which further cause one to be caught in samsara.

ALL CONTAMINATED PHENOMENA ARE IN THE NATURE OF SUFFERING

We misunderstand the suffering nature of contaminated phenomena and grasp at the idea that some genuine happiness, some real bliss, can be attained from them. Even when we are experiencing very uncomfortable feelings, we grasp at the phenomena which cause these feelings, and consider them to be by nature pleasurable. The wrong view which grasps at things as being pleasurable results in strong attachment and consequent actions to attain or maintain connection with them. Even insects go to great lengths to attain food for themselves and their offspring.

One strives to attain goals, but due to ignorance and delusion, one misunderstands the nature of what one is going to attain, and once attained, these things can bring us harm. When we strive for something without the resources to attain it, when we fall short of our goals, we instead achieve something we don't want. This also causes suffering.

Even if one is successful and attains something one strives for, the attainment of that thing is not something which will last. Its impermanent nature will eventually cause one to have to separate from what was desired.

The absence of an understanding of emptiness and selflessness can be seen in the belief that an independent 'I' exists, and that we need to gain pleasure and avoid pain for that self. This misapprehension then results in mistaken actions. The effort of samsaric beings therefore necessarily falls into one of the following three categories:

1) One strives to achieve something and succeeds, but it actually brings about suffering instead of happiness;
2) One strives to achieve something and fails, and experiences something which is not wanted as a result of one's efforts;
3) One strives to achieve something and succeeds, but due to the impermanent nature of the thing attained, one eventually has to separate from it.

ALL PHENOMENA ARE EMPTY AND SELFLESS

All Buddhist schools assert the selflessness of persons. The lower schools say there is no such thing as a substantially existent, self-sufficient 'I.' Even though it seems to each of us that there is an 'I' which exists as some sort of independent entity, there is no self which exists as something separate from and independent of the aggregates. The higher schools agree but consider this to be a coarse view of selflessness. The Prasangikas assert the most subtle form of selflessness. They say there is no such thing as an inherently existent 'I.' They also assert that this lack of inherent existence applies not just to persons, but also to phenomena. This is the view of emptiness. Emptiness means that phenomena do not exist in their own right and are merely imputed by conceptual thought.[6]

NIRVANA IS PEACE

Due to not understanding that we can liberate ourselves completely from suffering and the causes of suffering, we never attempt to achieve liberation (nirvana) which is genuine peace. Another misunderstanding is that some beings maintain that temporary happiness and some level of spiritual realization is perfect liberation. Thus they fail to achieve complete liberation from suffering and the causes of suffering.

TRUE ORIGINS

All true sufferings are said to exist within a state of possessing four characteristics: impermanence, suffering, emptiness and selflessness. All four of these characteristics are, by their very nature, forms of true suffering. Although the four characteristics are the actual nature of true sufferings, they are not generally understood. Most persons hold mistaken views about them.

The four wrong views which misunderstand the characteristics of true suffering arise from misunderstanding the attributes of true suffering (see Figure 4.3). They serve as true origins of suffering. The first, not understanding impermanence, leads to grasping at things as being permanent. The second, not understanding the suffering nature of things, comes to see objects as being pleasurable by nature. The third, not understanding emptiness of the self and aggregates, leads to grasping at the aggregates as being pure. Finally, not understanding selflessness leads to believing that a solid, independently established self exists. These four mistaken views are the true origins of delusion.

Characteristics of True Suffering	Wrong Views
1. Impermanence	1. Grasping at things as being static
2. Suffering nature of things	2. Seeing objects as pleasurable by nature
3. Emptiness	3. Grasping at the aggregates as being pure
4. Selflessness	4. Believing that a person exists in an independent, self-supporting way

Figure 4.3. True origins: wrong views associated with the four characteristics of true suffering

There are two categories of true origins—delusion and karma. These two serve as the true origins of suffering. The true origins of delusion have just been presented. In dependence upon having the true origins of delusion, one engages in mistaken actions. These actions constitute the true origins of karma (actions).

There are four aspects of true origins. The first aspect is that of a cause. The second aspect is that of an origin. The third is that of conditions. That is, karma and delusion acting together as cause and origin serve as the conditions which bring about samsara. The fourth aspect of true origins is that when karma and delusion as the cause, origin, and conditions of suffering become very strong, they become the complete, thorough cause of samsara.

True origins of delusion and karma act as the causes for samsara (the state of suffering). In dependence upon their acting as causes, suffering and the state of suffering arises. That is, they serve as the origins of suffering. In dependence upon having delusion and karma the first two act together to bring about suffering in manifest form. Finally, when these occur in a very powerful form, they actually generate suffering and the state of suffering.

If one thinks about the characteristics of true origins one will realize the disadvantages of having them within one's own continuum. They are the factors which lead ourselves and others to this unsatisfactory state of existence. The question which naturally arises is "Is there any way of becoming free from such a state?"

CONCLUSION

Ignorance is the very root of all the origins of suffering and samsara. The question then becomes "Is there any way to get rid of that ignorance?" If there were no way to do so, it would be better not to introduce people to these ideas about suffering or to say life is in the nature of suffering. Rather, it would be kinder just to let them be happy in their own situations. Suffering and its causes are explained only in the context of a way to abandon them.

If a poor family had no means to buy food, it would be better not to tell them their diet was really poor. However, if someone who did have the means to improve their diet was eating something which wasn't good for them, then it would be suitable to say, you shouldn't eat this, you should eat another type of food instead.

It is only because there is a way to abandon suffering and the causes of suffering that they are presented. Understanding the situation in samsara, and that there is a way to abandon it, will lead one to develop the wish to do so. One will develop the state of mind that wants to turn away from samsara, that dislikes one's present situation, that cannot bear the constant state of suffering. Once this very strong mind has been generated, if the practices have been presented, one will engage in the practices that can lead away from that state.

True origins and true suffering are presented because the whole of samsara is based upon a mind or minds that grasp at things which are not true. This, therefore, provides the basis for positing a way of becoming free from the state of samsara.

To get rid of ignorance, one meditates on selflessness. This will decrease the strength of delusion, and eventually eliminate the mind that is not in accordance with reality. The question then arises, "What happens then? Does one reach a state which is completely free from suffering? Does it lead to the end of the person's continuum?" All of that is uncomfortable to think about. This is said not to be the case. All that one gets rid of is the mistaken state of mind that is the cause of all suffering. Without the causes of suffering, the person will not experience the suffering. The person remains, but has rid himself or herself of a mistaken state of mind and the problems which ensue from that.

The first two Noble Truths have been explained from the perspective of the person caught in samsara. The last two Noble Truths, true cessations and true paths, are presented from the point of view of someone who is escaping or who has escaped from samsara. True cessations and true paths, which also have a cause and effect relationship, are discussed in the next chapter.

5 The Third and Fourth Noble Truths: True Cessations and True Paths

True suffering and true origins were explained from the point of view of someone caught in samsara. True cessations and true paths are explained from the opposite point of view, that of someone who is escaping or who has escaped from the state of suffering.

TRUE CESSATIONS

There are different levels of the ignorance which sees things (persons, self or phenomena) as existing from their own side. If one abandons the intellectually acquired level of this wrong view, it is said that the person has had a true cessation of never being reborn in lower states of existence. Having abandoned this level of delusion, the person reaches a true cessation and can be reborn only in higher, more pleasurable states of existence.

There is a more subtle, innate level of this wrong view. When one abandons this, one is said to have reached the state of liberation (freedom from suffering). This state is completely free from the sufferings of birth, aging, sickness and death. No more delusions are generated within one's mind. That is, the person is able to cease both delusion and the suffering which arises from delusion.

CHARACTERISTICS OF TRUE CESSATIONS

There are four characteristics of true cessations (see Figure 5.1). These are, first, the cessation of suffering, and second, peace. The third is the result of the first two taken together and is benefit for oneself and bliss or pleasure. Finally, the fourth is definite emergence.

The Tibetan term for definite emergence has two parts. One means to emerge or arise from something. Emergence thus refers to release from samsara. Its past tense form, *arisen from*, means transcendent. The other part, meaning *definite*, refers to the fact that once this has been accomplished one is definitely released. It is a final state.

In summary, the four characteristics of true cessations are (1) cessation, (2) peace, (3) benefit and pleasure, and (4) definite arisal, or definite emergence. This completes the discussion of the first three Noble Truths.

TRUE PATHS

In the analogy of the patient, the physician and the medicine, true paths are equivalent to the medicine. If patients thought that they were terminally ill, and the physician told them there was a medicine which would bring a cure, they would obviously be interested in taking it. If they had faith in the fact that if they attained true cessations it would lead to the end of suffering, they would obviously generate great interest in engaging in those practices. This in turn would lead them to true paths.

True paths are related to the four characteristics of true suffering. The four wrong views which serve as true origins arise from the attributes of true suffering. For example, the wrong view of impermanence is the first cause of suffering. Therefore, it is necessary to reverse those wrong views. We have to eliminate grasping at permanence and realize impermanence. This will lead to a state of liberation.

Secondly, we need to eliminate the feeling that objects are pleasurable, and see them as being in the nature of suffering, or misery. Thirdly, one needs to rid oneself of the wrong view and understand emptiness. That is, one needs to get rid of the wrong view that sees the self and the aggregates as being different things and therefore sees the self as having independent substantial existence. Finally, we have to rid ourselves of the notion that there is a self, and come to realize selflessness. In other words, the path consists of reversing the four attributes of true suffering.

True Suffering	True Origins	True Cessations	True Paths
Impermanence	Cause	Cessation	Path
Suffering	Origin	Peace	Knower
Emptiness	Condition	Benefit and Bliss	Achiever; What Achieves
Selflessness	Thorough Production	Definite Emergence	Definite Elimination

Figure 5.1. The sixteen attributes of the Four Noble Truths

The things which have to be realized are called the sixteen attributes of the path.[1] Realizing impermanence and the rest of the sixteen attributes *is* the path. Impermanence, emptiness and selflessness are said to be the most important attributes and are emphasized the most. Selflessness is the most important one of these.

PATH

Wisdom, the mind which directly realizes these sixteen attributes, is said to be the path of a superior being. If one can meditate upon these attributes (especially selflessness) and realize them directly, this will eventually lead to liberation. The question of how this can lead to liberation is answered in the following way. Ignorance is the root of suffering, in that it causes the delusions that keep us within the state of suffering. The mind, the wisdom that realizes selflessness, acts as the antidote to ignorance. Ignorance is the root of samsara.

KNOWER

The mind which realizes these sixteen points is said to be the path or true paths. The generation of this mind leads to the desired state of liberation. It is also called "that which knows." The mind realizing these sixteen attributes understands the two cause and effect relationships of true suffering and true origins, and of true cessations and true paths. It understands the ultimate nature of all the four paths included within the Four Noble Truths.

THE ACHIEVER

The mind which understands these points is also called that which achieves or that which attains. If one has generated this mind and constantly meditates, then it leads one to the state of liberation. It is the mind itself which brings the person to that state.

DEFINITE ELIMINATION

Definite elimination refers to the state in which the mind, the realization, gets rid of the delusion. It is the state of eliminating the delusions. One does not fall back from this state.

THE SIXTEEN ATTRIBUTES OF THE FOUR NOBLE TRUTHS

The sixteen attributes of the Four Noble Truths are presented in Figure 5.1. (See Appendix A for further clarification.) Engaging in these true paths, one takes the attributes as the object of meditation and continuously meditates upon them. One eventually has direct experience, realization of them. At that point the person continues to meditate on that direct realization. That continuous meditation will eventually lead to liberation, a state

which is free from suffering. This is true for both Hinayana and
Mahayana practitioners.

FOUNDATIONS OF THE PATH

Moral discipline, concentration and wisdom are basic founda-
tions for the path. Each is explained separately below.

MORAL DISCIPLINE

Moral discipline is the foundation for these realizations. If one
were not to engage in the practices of moral discipline, then one
would probably not be able to reach the state of direct realization. The analogy given is that of a lamp which needs both a
sufficient amount and quality of fuel in order to burn clearly for
any length of time. Moral discipline is necessary not only for the
first actual direct realization of these points, but also for improving that state. Superior moral discipline, over and above that of
simply abandoning the ten non-virtuous actions and engaging
in the ten virtuous actions, is required. Superior moral discipline
involves taking vows of a novice or fully ordained monk or nun,
or Bodhisattva, and observing these vows very strictly.

CONCENTRATION AND WISDOM

Superior practices of concentration and wisdom are needed in
addition to superior moral discipline. First one has to engage in
practices of wisdom. It is necessary to improve the level of understanding of what one already understands, and gain understanding of what one does not. Study, contemplation and de-
bate are used to remedy misunderstandings and create
understanding of the things that are important to know. These
are the practices of ordinary wisdom.

Ordinary concentration is based on understanding what one
should meditate on, then engaging in that meditation. Ordinary
practices of contemplation lead to the superior practice of concentration. Superior concentration leads to the ability to enter
into profound forms of analysis, which in turn lead to the generation of a superior form of wisdom.

Briefly stated, ordinary wisdom is followed by ordinary concentration which leads to superior concentration. Superior concentration in turn leads to superior wisdom. However, in reality they must be practiced together.

Wisdom provides the ability to analyze meanings, and so forth. Concentration is the mind which single-pointedly focuses without disruption upon the object that wisdom has found. It is the unbroken, continuous state of mind which is single-pointedly focusing on the object. Concentration is required to focus, to direct the attention and make the wisdom stable.

Wisdom and concentration must necessarily go together. Each enhances the other. If one has wisdom, but does not apply concentration, two faults arise. The first is that one lacks clarity with respect to the object, will not be able to focus on the object, and a great deal of distraction will occur. This mind will not be able to grasp the object well. The second fault is that the wisdom will lack power. It will not be a penetrating wisdom. However, if the practices of wisdom and concentration are combined, these two faults are overcome. Wisdom becomes clear and able to stay with its object without wandering and it becomes a powerful and penetrating wisdom.

In tantric practices of visualizing deities and channeling energies within the body, one engages in concentration to enhance those practices. One tries to bring the object to mind and focus on that object without straying from it. On the other hand, to gain a precise, clear understanding of the teachings, wisdom is required.

Wisdom is used for meditation on the sixteen attributes of the Four Noble Truths or on the practices of compassion and bodhicitta, the altruistic mind of enlightenment. Wisdom is used to discriminate what these things actually are. When one has gone through the analytical processes in order to be able to discriminate these, then one mainly uses concentration to gain a deeper understanding of them. The objects discriminated by wisdom become the focus of meditation. Through concentration, one becomes very familiar with them.

Superior Concentration
Eventually, a firm, steady form of concentration is attained. It is a mind which does not waiver toward its object. There is no danger of slipping into thinking about, or focusing on something else. This is termed calm abiding. This is superior concentration, and from the point when that is attained, all one's concentrations are said to be superior concentrations (if one continues the practice of focused meditation).

Superior Wisdom
During the time one is trying to attain the superior practices of wisdom and concentration, as one increases, the other diminishes in power. Therefore, it is necessary to alternate between the two. However, after one has attained calm abiding, then one attains a state of superior seeing. In this stage, wisdom and concentration can abide together without conflict. One has firm concentration, but is able to analyze within that concentration. This stage of superior seeing, sometimes called special insight, is the superior practice of wisdom.

THE FIVE PATHS

The five paths are the paths of Accumulation, Preparation, Seeing, Meditation and No-More-Learning. These are explained below.

PATH OF ACCUMULATION
The first of the five paths is called the Path of Accumulation. Calm abiding is attained during the time the practitioner is on the Path of Accumulation. Prior to this point the practitioner focuses on the subtle selflessness of persons, and eventually calm abiding is achieved.

PATH OF PREPARATION
The Path of Preparation occurs once the practitioner has attained calm abiding. Superior seeing and calm abiding are attained simultaneously. Superior seeing is the criterion for attainment

of the Path of Preparation. It is said that there is no degeneration after one has attained that state. Prior to this, one's practice, one's states of mind, the lack of correct conditions, can all adversely affect one's realizations. After attaining the Path of Preparation, one may experience the negative karma of past actions and undergo unpleasant states and so forth. However, the practitioner's level of realizations does not degenerate.

PATH OF SEEING

While on the path of preparation, the practitioner has a conceptual understanding of the selflessness of persons or emptiness. However, s/he still does not have a direct realization of it. Much effort is required to meditate again and again on the selflessness of persons. It is also necessary to accumulate a great deal of merit, which serves to strengthen and steady the practices of wisdom. Thus, it is necessary to practice both the wisdom meditating on the subject and those practices which accumulate merit. If this is done, eventually the practitioner will have a direct experience of emptiness. The person sees emptiness directly. At that point the person is said to have achieved the Path of Seeing.

Once a practitioner has attained the Path of Seeing, that person has reached a state where s/he will never ever fall back into lower states of rebirth. S/he will not be born into the lower realms powerlessly or without his or her own choice. S/he also does not accumulate karma which would act as the basis for being reborn in samsara. From the time a practitioner directly realizes emptiness and thereby attains the state of the Path of Seeing, that person is said to be a Superior Being. The Path of Seeing is the Path of a Superior Being (an Arya).

The practice on the Path of Seeing is simply to take as one's object the experience of the direct realization of emptiness, the selflessness of persons, and meditate on that again and again until one attains the Path of Meditation.

PATH OF MEDITATION

There are nine levels of the Path of Meditation. These consist of three levels—the great, the middling and the small—plus similar subdivisions of great, middling and small within each of these three. The practitioner gets rid of increasingly subtle layers of delusions while on this path. When the practitioner reaches the final, most subtle delusions, s/he is said to have achieved the state of liberation. This person is then termed a Foe Destroyer, or an Arhat.

PATH OF NO-MORE-LEARNING
Discussion of the Path of No-More-Learning can be found in other sources.[2]

SUMMARY OF THE PATHS
The selflessness of persons is first directly realized on the Path of Seeing. This realization becomes the focus of repeated meditation on the Path of Meditation. This path continues through the nine levels of delusion which must be overcome in order to achieve liberation. When the ninth and last level of delusion is overcome, one is said to have achieved liberation.

CONCLUSION

The Four Noble Truths present a comprehensive, interrelated description of the reality of suffering and the means to achieve the end of suffering. Ignorance, delusion and action produce the suffering which pervades sentient beings and their environment. Wisdom, concentration and moral discipline provide the clarity and force to overcome the origins of suffering, and with effort these practices can eventually lead to the cessation of suffering for self and others.

Appendix A
Sixteen Attributes of the Four Noble Truths

THE FOUR ASPECTS OF TRUE SUFFERINGS

1) Phenomena such as the physical and mental aggregates, because of their characteristic of undergoing continuous momentary production and disintegration, are *impermanent*.
2) As that process of change is impelled by karma and delusion, the aggregates have the nature of *suffering*.
3) Because there is no independent self which exists separately from the aggregates they are *empty*.
4) As they lack the existence of any type of self-supporting person, they are *selfless*.

THE FOUR ASPECTS OF TRUE ORIGINS

1) As suffering constantly arises from contaminated karma and delusion, karma and delusion have the quality of being the *causes*.
2) As all of the multifarious forms of suffering are produced by those two, they have the quality of being the *origin*.
3) Because they act forcefully as the causes for the production

of suffering, they have the quality of *strong production*.
4) Because they also act as the immediate conditions that give rise to suffering, they have the quality of being *conditions*.

THE FOUR ASPECTS OF TRUE PATHS

1) The wisdom directly realizing selflessness, due to being the unerring path to liberation, has the quality of being *the path*.
2) As that wisdom understands the nature of bondage in and release from samsara just as they are, it has the quality of *awareness*.
3) Because it achieves or secures the unerring path to liberation, it has the quality of *achievement*.
4) Because it destroys the main cause of samsara, it has the quality of *deliverance*.

THE FOUR ASPECTS OF TRUE CESSATIONS

1) As the absence of delusions, a state in which they have been abandoned, has the feature of ensuring that suffering will no longer be produced, it has the quality of *cessation*.
2) Because it pacifies the torment of suffering, it has the quality of *pacification*.
3) As it is the source of help and happiness, it has the quality of being *superb*.
4) Because it means total release from samsara, it has the quality of *definite emergence*.

Appendix B
The Five Paths

There are five respective paths: those of Accumulation, Preparation, Seeing, Meditation and No-More-Learning for each of the three types of practitioners—Hearers, Solitary Realizers and Bodhisattvas.

The Hearers' Path of Accumulation is their mainly engaging in practices of listening to and contemplating the meaning of the teachings for the sake of attaining the liberation of a hearer.

Their Path of Preparation is their emphasis on meditation on those meanings, as opposed to listening and contemplation.

Their Path of Seeing occurs when they see directly the nature of the Four Truths.

The period when they subsequently meditate on what they have directly understood is their Path of Meditation.

Then when they reach the completion of that meditation practice they have attained the path of No-More-Learning.

The process is similar for the Solitary Realizer and Bodhisattva practitioners except that the former's practices are aimed at achieving the liberation of a Solitary Realizer and the latter, the enlightenment of a Buddha.

Glossary

Aggregates. The constituents of a sentient being—form, feeling, discrimination, compositional factors and consciousness. Sentient beings in the formless realms, however, lack the first of these.

Arhat. Someone who has completely eradicated the delusions from his or her continuum.

Arya. A superior being. One who has directly realized selflessness and thereby attained the state of the Path of Seeing or above.

Calm abiding. A superior type of concentration, single-pointedly holding its object and undisturbed by the factors of sinking or excitement.

Compositional factors. The mental factors which tie the object with the mind, selecting the object of attention and maintaining that attention or changing the focus of attention. One of the five aggregates.

Concentration. The function of unbroken mental continuity single-pointedly focusing on an object. *Superior concentration* is the concentration in which the ability to analyze is not lost.

Consciousness. That which is clear and knowing.

Consciousness aggregate. There are six consciousnesses—five sense consciousnesses and one mental consciousness. Each sense consciousness is associated with its appropriate sense base.

Contaminated aggregates. Aggregates forged by the interaction of karma and delusion, which are thereby in the nature of suffering.

Delusion. Any mind which, once manifest, brings about the loss of any mental peace. Seeing things as other than they are. *Imputed, acquired delusions* are those distorted states of mind which are not present at birth but which are built up on the basis of incorrect tenet systems and fallacious reasoning.

Direct perception. That perception which places no intermediate concept or generic image between the perceiver and the perceived.

Discrimination. The mental factor which differentiates or distinguishes and understands an object without mistaking it for others. One of the five aggregates.

Emptiness. In the Prasangika Madhyamika system, the absence of inherent—self-supporting or self-powered—existence in any given phenomenon.

Feeling. Awareness which experiences pain, pleasure or neutral feelings. One of the five aggregates.

Five Paths. The paths of (1) Accumulation, (2) Preparation, (3) Seeing, (4) Meditation and (5) No-More-Learning.

Form aggregate. The physical body of beings, including flesh, blood, bone, etc. One of the five aggregates.

Four Seals. The four characteristics which constitute the main points differentiating Buddhist tenets from other systems of thought.

Ignorance. A mental state that actively misconstrues or lacks understanding of the nature of phenomena.

Impermanence. *Gross impermanence* refers to the changes which can be directly observed with the passage of time by undeveloped minds. *Subtle impermanence* refers to momentary changes which generally cannot be directly observed.

Inferential cognition. Knowledge which results from perfect reasoning and requires a generic image between the perceiver (mind or person) and the perceived.

Karma. Actions, classified as virtuous, non-virtuous or neutral, committed by means of body, speech or mind. *Completing karma* is that karma which results in the experiences within a rebirth. *Propelling karma* is that karma which throws one into a particular form of rebirth.

Liberation. The state in which delusions are absent. It is chiefly achieved through the successful completion of the Hinayana path of practice.

Mind of definite emergence. Renunciation, or a non-fabricated determination to get out of cyclic existence.

Path. A consciousness realizing subtle objects such as impermanence and the other fifteen attributes of the Four Noble Truths.

Samsara. The endless cycle of uncontrolled birth, death and interim state perpetuated by true origins and characterized by true suffering.

Superior seeing. Superior wisdom, that is, the ability to analyze which is also compatible with simultaneous firm concentration. Sometimes called special insight.

True cessations. The abandonment of the delusion that sees self or other phenomena as existing from their own side. Once present it ensures that no further delusions are generated within the mind.

True paths. The practices used to reverse true suffering and attain true cessations.

True suffering. Having the nature of suffering (though not necessarily the feeling of suffering). It includes (1) the suffering of suffering, (2) the suffering of change and (3) pervasive suffering.

Twelve links of dependent origination. One description of suffering which focuses on phases of the lifespan and development as cause and effect of the interaction between ignorance, actions and suffering.

Wisdom. An awareness which functions to analyze the qualities and characters of objects.

Notes

Chapter 1

1. *Contaminated aggregates* is the term used for the body and mind which are produced by karma and delusion. This and other technical terms are explained in the Glossary.
2. Lati Rinbochay and Elizabeth Napper, *Mind in Tibetan Buddhism* (Ithaca, NY: Snow Lion, 1980), p. 16.

Chapter 2

1. According to Tenzin Gyatso, the Fourteenth Dalai Lama, "In the formless realm all forms, sounds, odours, tastes and tangible objects and the five senses for enjoying them are absent; there is only mind, and beings abide in neutral feeling, one-pointedly and without distraction." *The Buddhism of Tibet*, translated by Jeffrey Hopkins (London: Unwin Hyman, 1975), p. 25.
2. Lati Rinbochay and Jeffrey Hopkins, *Death, Intermediate State and Rebirth* (Ithaca, NY: Snow Lion, 1980).

Chapter 3

1. See also His Holiness the Dalai Lama of Tibet, Tenzin Gyatso and Jeffrey Hopkins (trans. and ed.), *The Dalai Lama at Harvard* (Ithaca, NY: Snow Lion, 1980), pp. 77-79.

2. The aggregates of body and mind, with emphasis on the aspect of their constantly changing nature. See *The Dalai Lama at Harvard*, p. 87.

Chapter 4

1. *The Dalai Lama at Harvard*, pp. 88-89.
2. See Jeffrey Hopkins, *Meditation on Emptiness* (London: Wisdom, 1983), p. 281.
3. Bardo being: a being in the intermediate state. "It has the shape of the body of the next life, whether hell-being, hungry ghost, animal, human, demigod or god." *Death, Intermediate State and Rebirth*, p. 50. See also pp. 51-52.
4. *The Dalai Lama at Harvard*, p. 36.
5. *The Dalai Lama at Harvard*, pp. 36-37.
6. See also Ven. Lobsang Gyatso, *The Harmony of Emptiness and Dependent-Arising* (Dharamsala: Library of Tibetan Works and Archives, 1992).

Chapter 5

1. See *The Dalai Lama at Harvard*, pp. 36-88.
2. See, for example, *The Dalai Lama at Harvard*, Chapter 10; and His Holiness the Dalai Lama of Tibet, Tsong-ka-pa and Jeffrey Hopkins, *Deity Yoga* (Ithaca, NY: Snow Lion, 1981), pp. 229-34.

Index